Unshakeable Foundations
A Guide to Steady and Reliable Income Streams

Andrew Galowey

Copyright © [Andrew Galowey] [2024]. All rights reserved. No part of this publication may be reproduced, distributed, or transmitted in any form or by any means, including photocopying, recording, or other electronic or mechanical methods, without the prior written permission of the publisher, except in the case of brief quotations embodied in critical reviews and certain other noncommercial uses permitted by copyright law.

Table Of Contents

Introduction

Chapter 1: Establishing a Strong Foundation: Understanding Income Streams and Risk Management

Chapter 2: The Power of Passive Income: Exploring Long-Term Gains

Chapter 3: Dividend Payouts: Making Your Investments a Consistent Income Source

Chapter 4: Crafting a Balanced Portfolio: Diversification for Long-Term Returns

Chapter 5: Weathering the Storms: Strategies to Protect Your Income Streams During Economic Downturns

Chapter 6: Building Your Financial Future: Taking Action to Achieve Financial Security

Introduction

Have you ever imagined an income source as consistent and dependable as the sunrise? One that endures economic instability, offering stability and peace of mind? In "Unshakeable Foundations: A Guide to Steady and Reliable Income Streams," we'll go on a quest to create precisely that. This book is your guide to creating a financial future in which money continues to flow, even when the winds of economic change are howling.

We'll look at passive income techniques, the value of dividend-paying companies, and how to build a well-diversified portfolio that can weather any storm. Forget transitory fads and hazardous initiatives; instead, we concentrate on laying the groundwork for long-term revenue sources.

Whether you're just getting started in your financial path or want to strengthen an existing one, "Unshakeable Foundations" will provide you with the information and techniques you need to reach financial stability. Are you ready to create a future in which your income fluctuates in accordance with your desires rather than the market's? Let we begin.

Chapter 1: Establishing a Strong Foundation: Understanding Income Streams and Risk Management

Imagine a life in which revenue comes in on a continuous basis, moving you toward your financial objectives. This is not a pipe dream; with the appropriate techniques, it is a genuine possibility. "Unshakeable Foundations: A Guide to Steady and Reliable Income Streams" can help you construct a solid financial future.

This first chapter sets the basis by discussing revenue sources and their importance in financial stability. We'll look at the many sorts of revenue streams, understand the dangers connected with each, and provide you with the information to properly manage those risks.

The Cornerstone of Financial Freedom: Understanding Income Streams

There are three main ways revenue enters your life: earned income, passive income, and portfolio income.

Earned income is the most common; it is the cash you earn for your time and talent at work. This is the classic approach to financial security, but it has drawbacks. You exchange your time for money, and your income ends when you quit working.

In contrast, passive income continues to flow even while you are not actively working. Passive income sources include rental properties, royalties from creative works, and internet enterprises that need no continuous effort. The trick is to set up the system initially, and it will create cash over time.

Portfolio income is the result of putting your money in return-generating assets. This category includes dividend-paying equities and bonds, as well as real estate investment trusts (REITs). While portfolio income might be passive in the sense that it is not actively managed on a daily basis, it does need an initial investment and is subject to market risks.

Creating a solid financial future often requires a mix of these revenue sources. Earned income serves as the basis, while passive and portfolio income offer a safety net and pave the road for long-term financial stability.

Unmasking the Risks: Possible Threats to Your Income Streams

No revenue source is completely risk-free. Understanding these possible hazards is critical to developing a robust financial strategy. Let's take a deeper look at the hazards connected with each revenue stream type.

Earned income risk: Job loss, disability, or industry downturns may all interrupt your revenue stream.

- Passive income risk: Vacancies in rental properties, changes in customer behavior that influence internet enterprises, and variations in royalty revenue may all disrupt passive income sources.

- Portfolio income risk: Market downturns may result in lower stock prices and dividend distributions. Bond defaults and interest rate fluctuations may have an influence on portfolio income.

The key to reducing these risks is diversification. Don't depend on just one form of income. Divide your income across several categories and asset types to establish a cushion against unforeseen catastrophes.

Creating a Risk Management Arsenal
Now that we've covered the various revenue sources and their possible hazards, let's look at some ways for efficiently managing them:

- Emergency fund: Having an easily accessible emergency fund might serve as a safety net in the event of job loss or unforeseen costs. Aim to save 3-6 months of living costs.

- Investing in your skills and education may increase your value as an employee, lowering your chances of losing your job. Keep up with industry changes and learn new skills to stay competitive.

- Risk reduction for passive income: Do extensive study before investing in rental properties or internet enterprises. Diversify your passive revenue streams to decrease dependency on a single enterprise.

Portfolio diversification is spreading your assets over many asset types, such as stocks, bonds, and real estate. This reduces risk since various asset types respond differently to market changes.

- Asset allocation: Divide your investment portfolio according to your risk tolerance and time horizon. Younger investors with a longer time horizon are more risk tolerant and may devote a larger portion of their portfolio to equities. As you approach retirement, gradually convert your portfolio to more conservative investments, such as bonds.

- Risk management tools: Consider using stop-loss orders on equities to reduce possible losses during market downturns. Use portfolio rebalancing to achieve your desired asset allocation over time.

Understanding the various revenue sources, their associated hazards, and executing good risk management measures can help you construct a financial fortress. The next chapter digs into the interesting realm of passive income techniques, looking at several ways to produce money even while you are not actively working.

Chapter 2: The Power of Passive Income: Exploring Long-Term Gains

Imagine constant revenue, like a soft but steady rain, nurturing your financial well-being. This, in essence, is the allure of passive income. In this chapter, we will dig into the topic of passive income techniques, looking at numerous choices for creating consistent income streams that work for you even while you sleep.

Beyond the Paycheck: Revealing the Allure of Passive Income

Passive income is a tempting alternative to the typical salary paradigm. Here's what makes it appealing:

- Time Freedom: Unlike earned income, which involves trading time for money, passive income enables you to recover your time. Once the initial setup is complete, many revenue sources take little continuing work to sustain.

- Financial Security: Passive income diversifies your income streams, providing a safety net and decreasing your reliance on a single wage. This may be especially useful during economic downturns or times of job loss.

- Building Wealth: Passive income sources have the potential to generate enormous wealth over time. Reinvesting your money may help you develop wealth faster.

However, it is critical to moderate expectations. Passive income seldom results in sudden riches. Building a long-term passive income stream sometimes requires a significant initial commitment of time and work.

Exploring the Passive Income Landscape: A Look at Different Options

The good news is that there are several passive income methods to examine, each tailored to a certain skill set and interest. Here are a few common options:

Investing in rental properties has long been a tried-and-true method for generating passive income. Owning a rental property provides consistent rental income, and the property's value might rise over time. However, maintaining rental properties involves continuous work, including tenant screening, upkeep, and probable vacancy periods.

- Online Businesses: The digital era provides a plenty of passive income alternatives. Consider generating and selling online courses, ebooks, and printables. Other ideas include starting a blog using affiliate marketing or creating a subscription-based membership website. The idea is to build a useful online presence with a steady audience.

- Peer-to-Peer Lending: These platforms link you with borrowers in need of loans. You may invest in these loans and earn interest on your repayments. However, there is significant risk involved since borrowers may fail on their loans.

- Dividends: If you own dividend-paying stocks, you may receive a percentage of the earnings that a firm distributes to its shareholders. While not fully passive (research is required to choose dependable dividend companies), dividend income may be a consistent source of income over time.

- Royalties: If you are a creative person, try earning money via royalties. This may be publishing ebooks or songs, providing stock photographs or videos, or designing applications with recurring income. The trick is to develop high-quality, in-demand content that connects with your target audience.

Choosing the Right Path: Discovering Your Ideal Passive Income Strategy

The optimal passive income approach for you is determined by your unique circumstances, hobbies, and risk tolerance. Here are some aspects to consider before making your decision:

- Skills and Interests: Use your present abilities and hobbies. If you like writing, producing an ebook may be an excellent match. If you're tech-savvy, think about creating an app.

- Investment Capital: Some passive income solutions demand an initial investment, while others are more affordable. Consider how much you're willing to commit initially.

- Time Commitment: While passive income needs less continuous work than earned income, certain solutions require time to set up and maintain.

- Risk Tolerance: Some passive income solutions, such as peer-to-peer lending, have greater inherent risks. Select an option that matches your risk tolerance and comfort level.

The Road to Passive Income Success: Essential Tips for Getting Started

Building strong passive income sources needs effort and intelligent thinking. Here are some important points to bear in mind:

Before embarking on any passive income enterprise, do thorough study. Understand the market, the competitors, and any possible dangers.

- Start Small, Scale Gradually: Do not expect to develop a passive income empire overnight. Start small with one or two tactics and progressively expand as you acquire expertise and success.

- Focus on Quality: Whether it's an online course, an ebook, or a rental property, make sure your product is high-quality and adds value to your target audience.

- material is King: In the digital world, creating quality and interesting material is critical for attracting and maintaining an audience. Regularly update your services to remain current in your selected area.

- Be Patient and Persistent: Generating passive income requires time and effort. Do not get disheartened by first setbacks. Be persistent, tweak your techniques, and continue to learn.

Chapter 3: Dividend Payouts: Making Your Investments a Consistent Income Source

Have you ever imagined your assets working for you, providing a continuous source of income? Look no farther than stocks that pay dividends! This chapter delves into the subject of dividends and how they may become a consistent source of income in your overall financial plan.

Unveiling the Dividend Powerhouse: Understanding how dividends work

Companies are not required to share their earnings with shareholders, although many well-established and lucrative businesses do. Dividends are a percentage of a company's profits that are paid out to its shareholders, usually quarterly. The amount paid per share is chosen by the board of directors and may change based on the company's performance and future goals.

The Allure of Dividends: Advantages of Holding Dividend-Paying Stocks

Dividend-paying equities provide numerous appealing benefits for investors seeking consistent income:

Dividends offer a constant and predictable flow of income, augmenting your earning income or functioning as a retirement income source.

- Hedge Against Inflation: Over time, inflation reduces the buying power of your money. Dividend-paying equities may assist to reduce this impact. Companies that continuously boost dividends may provide an increasing revenue stream that keeps up with inflation.

- Investment Growth Potential: While dividend payments offer current income, the underlying equities have the potential to increase in value over time. This may result in substantial gains when you sell the shares.

- **Market Volatility Buffer:** Dividend-paying stocks are often from mature, established corporations with a proven track record of success. These firms are often less volatile than the overall market, providing some protection during economic downturns.

However, dividends are not without downsides. Here are some important considerations:

- **Not guaranteed:** Companies are not required to pay dividends. Dividends may be reduced or suspended entirely at the discretion of the board.

- **Tax implications:** Dividends are normally treated as ordinary income, which means they are taxed at your standard marginal tax rate.

Dividend-paying stocks may provide lower total returns than high-growth equities, since corporations reinvest a smaller portion of their income for future development.

Choosing the Right Dividend Stock: Creating a Strong Dividend Portfolio

Not all dividend stocks are made equal. Here's how to choose companies that can become consistent sources of income for your portfolio:

- Dividend Payment History: Look for firms that have a lengthy and consistent history of paying dividends, demonstrating a commitment to shareholder returns.

- Dividend Yield: This measure calculates the yearly dividend payout as a proportion of the stock's price.

While a high yield is appealing, choose firms with sustainable dividend distributions above those that provide unsustainable high yields.

- Financial Strength: Look for organizations with a robust balance sheet, stable profitability, and low debt levels. Such corporations are more likely to sustain dividend payments over time.

- rise Potential: Look for firms that have a good blend of steady dividend distributions and potential for future stock price rise.

Remember, diversity is essential. Do not put all your eggs in one basket. To reduce risk, diversify your assets across industries and firms.

Beyond the Fundamentals: Advanced Strategies for Dividend Investors

For experienced investors looking to optimize their dividend income, here are some advanced techniques to consider:

- Dividend Reinvestment Plans (DRIPs): Many firms provide DRIPs, which enable you to automatically reinvest dividends in additional shares of stock. Compounding may help increase your portfolio's growth.

- Focus on Dividend Aristocrats: These are firms that have grown their dividends for at least 25 years in a row. They are a limited group of financially healthy corporations dedicated to repaying shareholders.

- High-Dividend ETFs and Mutual Funds: Exchange-Traded Funds (ETFs) and mutual funds that specialize on dividend-paying equities provide immediate diversification and expert management of your dividend portfolio.

The Road to Dividend Success: Essential Tips for Establishing a Reliable Income Stream

Building a profitable dividend portfolio needs meticulous preparation and a long-term mindset. Here are some important pointers to remember:

- Conduct Thorough Research: Before investing in a dividend-paying stock, look at the company's finances, dividend history, future growth possibilities, and general business plan.

- Don't chase high yields; instead, look for firms that send out reliable dividends. High yields might be appealing, but they may not be sustainable in the long term.

- Invest for the Long Term: Dividend investing is a long-term approach. Do not anticipate speedy results. Patience and a long-term investing view are critical to success.

Regularly monitor your portfolio to be updated about the firms in which you invest. Monitor their financial performance, dividend distribution adjustments, and any news that may affect their future.

Chapter 4: Crafting a Balanced Portfolio: Diversification for Long-Term Returns

Consider your financial future not as a shaky house of cards, but as a strong, well-diversified portfolio - a fortress constructed to weather economic storms. This chapter digs into the notion of portfolio diversity, which is a key factor for obtaining sustainable and predictable returns.

Beyond a Single Basket: Why Diversification is Key

The financial world is fundamentally unpredictable. Markets change, sectors may collapse, and even the most promising businesses can fail. Diversification is the solution to this uncertainty. It is the practice of diversifying your assets across asset classes, lowering your total risk and boosting your chances of meeting your financial objectives.

Understanding the Building Blocks: Exploring Different Asset Classes.

Consider your portfolio as a mosaic, with each tile representing a distinct asset type. When establishing a diversified portfolio, examine the following main asset classes:

Stocks signify ownership in a company. They have the potential for significant financial appreciation, but also pose a greater risk owing to market volatility.

Bonds are simply loans given to governments or enterprises. They provide a steady income stream in the form of interest payments and are typically seen as less volatile than equities.

Cash equivalents include money market accounts and short-term certificates of deposit. They provide poor profits but give liquidity and security for your money.

Real estate investment may be either direct (property ownership) or indirect (via REITs). It may provide revenue via rentals and capital appreciation, but it also has some hazards, including as vacancy periods and maintenance expenditures.

- Alternative Investments: This group includes a broader variety of assets, such as commodities (gold and oil), hedge funds, and private equity. While they may provide substantial profits, they also involve considerable risk and sometimes need a higher minimum commitment.

Finding Your Balance: Asset Allocation Strategies for Diverse Goals

The optimal asset allocation for your portfolio is determined by various variables, including your age, risk tolerance, and financial objectives. Here's an overall framework to consider:

- Younger Investors: Younger investors with a longer time horizon may often bear higher risk. They may invest a larger share of their portfolio to equities for prospective growth, while keeping bonds and cash equivalents to a minimum.

- Middle-Aged Investors: As you reach middle age, your risk tolerance may drop, so consider changing your portfolio allocation. Increase your bond allocation gradually for stability and income, while keeping a balanced stock portfolio for long-term gain.

- Nearing Retirement: As retirement approaches, emphasize money preservation above ambitious growth. Increase your exposure to bonds and cash equivalents to secure a consistent income stream and safeguard your nest egg.

Beyond the Basics: Advanced Diversification Techniques

While asset class diversity is important, you may improve your portfolio's resilience by using more sophisticated techniques:

- Sector Diversification: Spread your stock holdings across many industries, including as technology, healthcare, and consumer staples. This lessens your reliance on the success of any one industry.

- Geographic Diversification: Avoid limiting your assets to your own nation. Invest in foreign equities and funds to reduce the risks linked with a particular geographic region's economic collapse.

- Company Size Diversification: Incorporate a mix of large-cap (established firms), mid-cap (medium-sized companies), and small-cap (growth-oriented enterprises) stocks into your portfolio. This enables the exploitation of multiple development possibilities at various phases of a company's lifespan.

Rebalancing for Long-Term Success: Maintaining Balance in Your Portfolio

Market volatility may lead your asset allocation to deviate from your initial strategy. For example, if the stock market soars, the proportion of equities in your portfolio will rise. Rebalancing is returning your portfolio to its desired asset allocation by purchasing or selling assets as required. Regular rebalancing of your portfolio helps to maintain your chosen risk profile and assures long-term success.

Building a Balanced Portfolio: Key Takeaways

Diversification is the foundation of a sound and dependable investing plan. By diversifying your assets across asset classes, industries, and geographic locations, you lower risk while increasing your chances of meeting your financial objectives. Remember that asset allocation methods are personal. When creating your portfolio, keep in mind your age, risk tolerance, and financial objectives. Monitor your portfolio on a regular basis and rebalance as required to maintain your desired degree of diversity and protect your assets from the inevitable storms of the financial markets.

The next chapter will go over ways for maintaining your revenue streams during economic downturns, providing you with the information you need to secure your financial well-being.

Chapter 5: Weathering the Storms: Strategies to Protect Your Income Streams During Economic Downturns

Economic downturns are a natural component of the financial cycle. While they may generate concern, with the appropriate solutions in place, you can secure your revenue sources and emerge stronger. This chapter provides you with the necessary skills to handle economic upheaval and protect your financial well-being.

Understanding Threats: How Downturns Impact Income Streams

Economic downturns emerge in a variety of ways, any of which might pose a danger to your revenue streams:

- Market Volatility: During a recession, stock prices might fall, lowering the value of your portfolio and possibly cutting dividend payments from equities.

- Job Losses: In reaction to the economic recession, businesses may adopt layoffs or hiring freezes, putting your earnings at risk.

- Reduced Consumer Spending: During a recession, consumer spending falls, possibly hurting revenue from passive sources such as rental homes or web enterprises.

Building a Fortress: Strategies to Protect Your Income Streams

The key to surviving economic downturns is taking proactive steps to enhance your financial foundation. Here are some important methods to consider:

An emergency fund provides a necessary safety net during times of economic distress. Aim to save 3-6 months of living expenditures to cover unforeseen bills or income fluctuations.

- Debt Management: When circumstances are tough, high-interest debt may put a burden on your budget. Prioritize paying off high-interest debt, such as credit cards, and avoid taking on new debt during times of economic instability.

Investing in your skills and education may increase your value as an employee, so enhancing your job security. Stay current with industry trends and learn new skills to stay competitive in the employment market.

- Diversify Your Income Streams: Avoid relying exclusively on one source of income. Explore and establish several revenue sources, such as a side business or passive income opportunities, to provide a safety net and lessen reliance on a single source.

- Recession-Proof assets: Some assets provide better stability during a recession. Consider include government bonds, utility companies, or consumer staple stocks in your portfolio since they tend to retain their value better than other assets during economic downturns.

Strategies to Reduce Losses

Even with planning, economic downturns may bring financial hardship. Here's how to handle a slump while minimizing the effect on your revenue streams:

- Review Your Budget: Evaluate your spending patterns and discover places where you might reduce money. To withstand the financial storm, prioritize critical costs while reducing frivolous spending.

- Renegotiate Debts: If you're having trouble making your debt payments, contact your creditors to explore lower interest rates or longer payback periods.

- improve Your Side Hustle: If you have a side hustle, look into strategies to improve your revenue from it. Utilize your abilities and look into freelancing employment or internet platforms to complement your income.

- Tap into Your Emergency Fund: If you lose your job or have a major income loss, your emergency fund may give critical financial assistance until you find new work or restore your financial footing.

- Invest Strategically: While the stock market may be turbulent during a recession, you should not panic and sell your assets at a loss. Consider dollar-cost averaging, which involves investing a predetermined amount at regular intervals regardless of market swings. This allows you to acquire additional shares at cheap prices and average your costs over time.

Lessons From losses

Economic downturns, although stressful, may also serve as spurs for beneficial development. Use this opportunity to review your financial objectives, improve your risk management tactics, and lay a more solid financial foundation. Here are several important takeaways:

- Financial Preparedness is Critical: Having a good financial plan that includes an emergency fund and several income sources considerably lowers the effect of economic downturns.

- Adaptability is Essential: Be prepared to adjust your spending patterns and money creation tactics when the economy changes.

- Learning Never Stops: Economic downturns teach us vital lessons about risk management and the need of developing a solid financial plan.

The road to financial security is a continuous one

Financial stability is a marathon, not a sprint. Diversifying your income sources, establishing a safety net, and modifying your methods throughout economic downturns will help you improve your financial foundation and emerge stronger from any financial crisis.

The last chapter of this book will inspire you to take action and turn these techniques into a specific strategy for reaching financial stability and creating a future in which your money flows continuously, regardless of economic circumstances.

Chapter 6: Building Your Financial Future: Taking Action to Achieve Financial Security

Imagine a world in which money flows freely, allowing you to follow your ambitions and live life on your own terms. This last chapter provides you with the information and incentive to take action, transforming the ideas discussed in this book into a specific blueprint for reaching unwavering financial stability.

From Knowledge to Action: Setting Your Financial Plan in Motion

Understanding financial principles is critical, but actual growth requires action. Here are the important stages for transforming the information in this book into a specific financial plan:

- Set SMART financial goals: Specificity is essential. Define your financial objectives explicitly, making them specific, measurable, attainable, relevant, and time-bound. Do you wish to retire earlier? How can you get $1,000 in passive income every month? Clearly outline your objectives and establish reasonable deadlines for attaining them.

- Take stock of your existing financial situation. To calculate your net worth, remove your obligations (debts) from your assets. Analyze your revenue and spending to better understand your financial flow. This self-awareness is essential for developing a strong financial strategy.

- Prioritize Debt Repayment: High-interest debt is a major impediment to financial stability. Create a debt repayment strategy that targets high-interest bills first, freeing up more income for savings and investments.

- Build Your Emergency Fund: Set aside 3-6 months' worth of living costs in a readily accessible emergency fund. This safety net protects you from unforeseen financial problems and gives you peace of mind.

- Diversify Your revenue sources: Investigate and build various revenue sources to lessen reliance on one source. Consider starting a side business, using passive income methods, or negotiating a raise at your existing employment. The more revenue sources you have, the stronger your financial base grows.

- Design your investing plan based on your risk tolerance, time horizon, and financial objectives. Diversify your portfolio across several asset types such as equities, bonds, and real estate. Rebalance your portfolio on a regular basis to ensure that your intended asset allocation is maintained.

- Automate Your Finances: Make automated transfers for savings, bill payments, and investment contributions. Automating these operations promotes consistency and lowers the likelihood of missing payments or investment opportunities.

Financial planning is a continuous activity that should be monitored and reassessed on a regular basis. Monitor your progress on a regular basis, reassess your objectives, and make any necessary adjustments to your tactics. Economic factors, life events, and your own shifting objectives may need changes to your strategy.

Building financial security requires time and effort

Creating financial stability is a marathon, not a sprint. There will be obstacles and temptations on the path. Here are some ways to remain motivated and dedicated to your financial goals:

- Milestones: Recognize and appreciate your accomplishments, no matter how large or tiny. Completing a debt payback plan or meeting a savings goal are accomplishments to be proud of.

- Seek Support: Surround yourself with supportive people who share your financial goals. Talk about your objectives with friends, family, or even a financial counselor.

- Educate Yourself Continuously: The financial world is continuously changing. Stay informed about investing trends, tax restrictions, and new possibilities. Continuous learning keeps your financial tactics current and successful.

- Focus on Progress, Not Perfection: Do not get disheartened by minor failures. Everyone make errors. The idea is to learn from them and keep focused on achieving your financial objectives.

Financial security is a path to freedom and empowerment

Financial stability is more than simply amassing riches. It's about achieving independence, control, and peace of mind. When you have a consistent source of income and a solid financial foundation, you can follow your goals, weather life's obstacles, and live a full life on your own terms.

Embrace the path, take action, and create a secure financial future. You already have the ability to reach financial stability!

50

www.ingramcontent.com/pod-product-compliance
Lightning Source LLC
Chambersburg PA
CBHW070924220526
45470CB00012B/2127